PREACHING
— *that* —
GETS THROUGH

God's Word and our words

Stuart Olyott

THE BANNER OF TRUTH TRUST

THE BANNER OF TRUTH TRUST
3 Murrayfield Road, Edinburgh EH12 6EL, UK
PO Box 621, Carlisle, PA 17013, USA

*

© The Banner of Truth Trust 2011

ISBN: 978 1 84871 141 9

*

Typeset in 11/15 pt Adobe Garamond Pro at
The Banner of Truth Trust
Printed in the USA by
Versa Press, Inc.,
East Peoria, IL.

*

All Scripture quotations are taken from
The Holy Bible, New King James Version
Copyright © 1982 Thomas Nelson, Inc.

INTRODUCTION

The Martyn Lloyd-Jones Memorial Lecture is an annual event sponsored by the John Owen Centre for Theological Study, London. In September 2010 I was privileged to be the lecturer and, apart from some introductory remarks, this booklet contains the substance of what I had to say. Readers who would like a recording of the lecture on CD or in MP3 format should either e-mail London Theological Seminary at admin@ltslondon.org or write to the Seminary at 104 Hendon Lane, London, NW3 3SQ (Tel: 020 8346 7587).

All of us who hear preaching are aware that some of it gets through and that some of it does not. Why is this? What, if anything, can preachers do to communicate more effectively? And can this be done without degrading the glory of the gospel message, or detracting from it? It is my hope and prayer that this booklet, like the original lecture, may be of some help to those who are wrestling with these questions.

STUART OLYOTT,
Connah's Quay,
North Wales,
February 2011.

PREACHING *that* GETS THROUGH

God's Word and our words

Our friend Adamu had taken a night flight from Nigeria to Britain and was disappointed that he had not seen the sea. My wife and I therefore took him for a visit to the coast. As he stood in awe gazing at the blue horizon, an unexpected wave struck the small cliff on which we were standing, throwing a great sheet of water and spangled droplets high into the air above him. In terrified wonder he cried out, 'I've seen the sea! I must tell my wife and children about this!'

He had seen the ocean! But how much of it had he seen? It did not matter. He knew that he had experienced a life-changing moment, a milestone in his life, and that his thinking about some matters could never be quite the same again.

The subject of *Preaching that Gets Through* is an ocean. It is vast. In a booklet such as this we can only consider the smallest part of it. All I can hope for is that one wave will leap up before you and that reading what follows will turn out to be a milestone in your life. It will be this if it succeeds in pointing out to you some ways in which preaching can change for the better.

So how shall we approach the subject? We will start with a quiz. We will look at seven statements and ask whether they are true or false. This will get us thinking.

Then we will need to say a little about Aristotle. Yes, we will! This is because there are many things that we can learn from him, while also recognising that much of what he taught is either untrue or unhelpful. In particular, we will need to be aware that there is one area on which he can shed no light at all. As the ministry of the Apostle Paul will help us to evaluate Aristotle, we will call this second section 'Aristotle and Paul'.

Thirdly, I am going to introduce you to what we call 'Upside-Down Thinking', because this may be the best way of clarifying what we will learn and of bringing it home to us. We will apply this way of thinking to four crucial areas (which we will have identified previously) and so be able to come to a practical conclusion about *Preaching that Gets Through*.

1. TRUE OR FALSE?

Let us, then, consider seven statements. Before you read what is said about each one, please take a moment to weigh up whether the statement is true or false.

(i) *Words are powerful things*

This is true. Of course it is! It is by *words* that:

- God spoke the universe into existence.
- The serpent tempted Eve, and caused her and Adam to fall.
- God announced the curse, but also promised the coming Saviour.
- All the prophets unveiled God's mind to Old Testament Israel.
- All generations have sung God's praise and addressed him in prayer.
- The Lord Jesus Christ spoke like no other person has ever spoken.
- The early church spread the gospel in the world.
- All preachers have ever conveyed their God-given message.

And, lest it be thought that we are speaking only about the use of words in biblical and Christian contexts, let us underline that words are powerful things wherever they may be found. For example, it was by words that Adolf Hitler stirred a nation to go to war, and it was by words that Winston Churchill rallied a nation to resist him!

(ii) Words are units of writing which are the smallest meaningful elements of the language that we can isolate, and which may or may not be spoken.

This booklet is about preaching; it is not a manual on linguistics. In making the statement above, therefore, I am leaving aside the whole question of morphemes. What we need to know is that the statement is false! It should read, 'Words are units of speech which are the smallest meaningful elements of the language that we can isolate, and which may or may not be written.'

Grasping this—really grasping it—is one of the key differences between being a preacher and being a mere speaker or lecturer. It is for this reason that almost all great preachers have preached from notes (or with no notes at all), rather than from a full manuscript. Words are spoken. Written words are simply symbols by which real words are remembered. Martyn Lloyd-Jones therefore, like C. H. Spurgeon[1] before him, only carried into the pulpit a small piece of paper on which was written just enough information to guide him safely through his sermon. Discerning readers will also have noted that the examples of the power of words contained in the first section above are all references to the spoken word. The written record has been given to us so that we do not forget.

---

[1] Charles Haddon Spurgeon (1834-1892) was the most influential gospel preacher of his age. His regular congregation at the Metropolitan Tabernacle, London, numbered many thousands, while many millions of copies of his printed sermons went all over the world. These, and his numerous other written works, are still widely read today.

(iii) Words are powerless to raise the spiritually dead unless they are accompanied by the omnipotent energy of the Holy Spirit.

This is true. This is the obvious implication of 1 Thessalonians 1:5-6. In these verses the Apostle Paul reflects on his preaching in Thessalonica by which he first brought the gospel message there. He writes:

> For our gospel did not come to you in word only, but also in power, and in the Holy Spirit, and in much assurance, as you know what kind of men we were among you for your sake. And you became followers of us and of the Lord, having received the word in much affliction, with joy of the Holy Spirit.

Paul makes it clear that it is possible for the gospel to come to people 'in word only'. He does not attribute the conversion of the Thessalonians to the simple fact that they had heard the message. No, no! Words, even gospel words, cannot on their own produce a spiritual change in anyone. The message must certainly come to people, but it must be 'in power, and in the Holy Spirit'.

Words can do a great deal, but they cannot regenerate. They cannot bring about the miracle of the new birth. They cannot renew a single heart. They cannot alter human nature. No one can say that Jesus is the Lord, except by the Holy Spirit. It is only by the spiritual transformation, the heavenly baptism, brought about by the 'one Spirit' that anyone can be made a member of the body of Christ (see *1 Cor.* 12:3, 13).

Words can inform, excite, move, thrill, enthuse and impassion people. But even if they are words of learning and taste, woven together with rhetorical skill, homiletically perfect, filled with reasoning and proof, sparkling in beauty, helped along by metaphor and narrative, and delivered by a prince of the pulpit, they are powerless to bring about spiritual change.

Something else is needed, and this Martyn Lloyd-Jones saw clearly. How we need to be equally clear about this today! Countless modern preachers, in line with many on the Lutheran side of the Reformation, nurse the conviction that if they simply expound the truth God's work will get done. This error must not be allowed to live a moment longer.

(iv) This said—as we use words, there are ways of getting through and ways of not getting through; and these are appointed by God.

This is true. This is why, in one instance, it is written of Paul and Barnabas that they 'so spoke that a great multitude both of the Jews and of the Greeks believed' (*Acts* 14:1).

The power which gives preaching success is supernatural. Nonetheless, there are what Henry Fish calls, 'Efficient modes of preaching the gospel, and inefficient modes.'[2] There are such things as laws of persuasion; that is, there are certain ways of speaking that influence the mind, and certain ways of speaking that do not influence the mind.

The Greeks knew this. This is why they laid such stress on rhetoric—which is a subject to which we will return. This is also why the crowds spoke so favourably of our Lord, being aware that he got through to them in a way that their rabbis never did.

---

[2] Fish, Henry C., *Power in the Pulpit*, (London, Banner of Truth, undated), p. 2.

At the end of the Sermon on the Mount we read:

> And so it was, when Jesus had ended these sayings, that the people were astonished at his teaching, for he taught them as one having authority, and not as the scribes (*Matt.* 7:28-29).

History also testifies to the existence of these laws of persuasion. For example, on Thursday 19th November, 1863 a great assembly of ordinary people and dignitaries gathered at Gettysburg, Pennsylvania, where countless men had perished at one of the decisive battles of the American Civil War. The occasion was the dedication of the new Soldiers' National Cemetery. A national figure and well-known speaker, Edward Everett, was invited to give the formal Oration. It was then understood that President Abraham Lincoln would say a few words.

Today the name of Edward Everett is largely forgotten. His 'Gettysburg Oration' was over 13,600 words long and lasted more than two hours. Most people have never heard of it and know nothing about it. The same cannot be said of President Lincoln's contribution. It was composed of about 260 words and lasted a little over two minutes, and yet it shaped the thinking of an entire nation for over one hundred years! Even today people talk frequently about 'The Gettysburg Address', and thousands of people know it off by heart.

There are, most certainly, laws of persuasion that influence the human mind. Almost all of us can recall sermons or speeches that have changed us for ever. We can also call to mind occasions when we were bored beyond description, while the person speaking at the front seemed to go on and on.

Why is this? It is because of the way in which God has constructed the human soul. It is true that that soul, like everything else about us, has been spoiled and perverted by the Fall. But it has not been destroyed. Nor has it been changed into something else. Despite all that the Fall has done to it, the human soul still exists and still bears the marks of its original construction. It remains a fact that certain ways of speaking get through to it, and other ways do not.

(v) *These ways of getting through can be learned*

This is true. It is still possible to analyse any speech and to notice that speeches which have certain characteristics get through, while those speeches that lack those characteristics do not get through.

What is true of any speech is certainly true of biblical speeches. We cannot literally hear the Old Testament prophets, or our Lord Jesus Christ, or the New Testament apostles. But we can read what they said, analyse how they said it, draw conclusions from our analysis, and learn lessons for ourselves.

Nor do we need to confine our study to the written records of biblical speeches, because we can listen 'live' to men who expound the Scriptures today, and apply our critical faculties to the study of how they do it. Some men preach badly; others do it better; while yet others preach well. We can learn from them all. A critical spirit is the Devil's invention and is something that we turn our back on; but a critical faculty is God's gift to us, and is something that he expects us to exercise. Some things are better than others, and he wants us to be able to recognise which is which. This is also true of the sermons that we hear. It is by exercising their critical faculties that godly men have given us so many helpful books on homiletics, one of which, of course, is *Preaching and Preachers* by Martyn Lloyd-Jones. Nobody would write a book on homiletics unless they believed that ways of getting through can be learned.

(vi) However, the Holy Spirit is no more likely to accompany these ways of getting through than those of not getting through.

This is false! God is indeed sovereign, but he is not arbitrary. Even when it comes to the work of grace in the human heart, there is a connection between the means used and the end achieved.

May I ask you if you believe this? Do you accept that words which affect someone without the Spirit may be expected to be the sort of words that would be used by the Spirit in carrying conviction to the human heart? Do you agree that the influences of the Holy Spirit are more likely to accompany words which observe the God-given rules of persuasion than those which do not observe those rules?

If this were not so, it would not matter at all—no, not ever!—how we spoke. It would be a matter of complete indifference. We could throw ideas and words together in a tangled and meaningless jumble, and still expect God to do his work through the verbal chaos that poured or stuttered out of our mouths. But the Bible never gives us the impression that that is what God wants; and no powerful preacher in history—and certainly not Martyn Lloyd-Jones—has ever believed that that is the way forward.

(vii) Our study of this subject can therefore be limited to two areas—that of considering what is to be preached—and that of considering how it is to be preached.

This is false, as will become clear as we continue through this booklet. Suffice it to say at this point that our study will have to embrace four areas. To get us on the way to doing that, let us now move to our second section.

2. ARISTOTLE AND PAUL

Aristotle, the Greek philosopher and scientist, lived from 384 B.C. to 322 B.C. A student of Plato, he later taught at his Academy in Athens. It was there that he met Alexander the Great, whom he tutored from the age of thirteen upwards. Eventually, with generous help from Alexander, Aristotle set up his own school, the Lyceum, which was also a research institute, a library and a museum.

Aristotle wrote about 400 books, on every conceivable subject, about one hundred of which still survive. Most of these books were probably never intended for publication, having been written simply as study notes for his students.

Why then, in a book on preaching, are we mentioning Aristotle? What do the studies of a pagan philosopher have to do with us? The answer is that one of his books is called *The Art of Rhetoric,* or, as some translate it, *The Art of Persuasion.* It is a book about persuasive public speaking that has influenced all thinking and writing on the subject from Aristotle's day to ours. Everybody who thinks, writes or speaks about public speaking has to interact with Aristotle, and that includes us!

Aristotle's book is in fact three books, and some of it is quite complicated. For example, he makes a distinction between atechnic and entechnic persuasion. He talks about rhetoric as deliberative, forensic and epideictic. He discusses enthymemes, lysis, syllogisms, rhythm, narration, epilogues, and countless other themes, in a way which leaves us baffled. What has all this to do with the man who has been set apart by Christ to preach his Word?

We would be foolish if we dismissed Aristotle. This is because he observed that whenever a public speaker gets through—really gets through—there are three things that you can notice about the whole experience. Over 2,300 years later, we can say that this is still the case, as almost everyone who has written or spoken on the subject of public speaking in all the intervening centuries freely acknowledges! Using Aristotle's words we can say that every compelling public speaker is characterised by *ethos, pathos* and *logos*. This is always the case. There are no exceptions. So, in using these terms, what did Aristotle mean?

Ethos

Today we use the word *ethos* in a way that Aristotle would not have recognised. For example, we talk about the *ethos* of an organisation or a place of work. We use the word to describe the ambiance or atmosphere prevailing among a group of people who are working together.

In his writings Aristotle uses the word *ethos* in a completely different way. He is not talking about something characterising a group of people, but about a quality projected by an individual. For example, when we go to hear a person speak in public we often know something about him beforehand. As a result, we have a certain perception of that person, which may or may not be accurate. We go to hear him either with some expectancy or with some hesitation, or even cynicism. The speaker's *ethos* affects how much attention we decide to give him, and also whether we will take him seriously or not.

Imagine two people being invited to give a public lecture on 'Walking on the Moon', one of which is Neil Armstrong and the other is your neighbour next door. It is obvious which one would command your attention. When we sit down to listen to someone speak, we expect him to have some credibility. He must speak with authority, as a person who knows what he is talking about. We want to see some evidence that he has a good mind, and that what he says is backed up by solid learning. We want to be sure that his previous study and experience give him a level of expertise in the area that he is talking about.

But what if we have never heard of the speaker before? In this case ethos is, perhaps, even more important. Does he look the part? Is the note of authority there? Does his demeanour enforce his message or contradict it? Do his personal allusions, and the content and organisation of his material, convince us that he has the right to be speaking on this subject? *Ethos* is all-important. It is a simple fact that people will listen to someone who they are reasonably convinced has something worthwhile to say to them. Some modern writers refer to *ethos* as 'ethical appeal'.

Pathos

Pathos refers to the observation that the speaker is absorbed with his audience. He respects his hearers and wishes them well. He puts himself in their shoes. He sets out to arouse their interest, often by stories or life incidents, and so takes them out of the realm of the abstract to the point where they feel that what he is saying is relevant to them.

The speaker with *pathos* stimulates the imagination of his hearers. He stirs them to belief and action. He displays feeling, not only about what he says, but for the people in front of him. It is clear to all that he is concerned for their welfare, and deeply aware of their beliefs, interests and goals. It is a simple fact that people will listen to someone who feels what he is saying and cares about his hearers. Some modern writers refer to *pathos* as 'emotional appeal'.

Logos

Logos refers to the speaker's content. He has something to say. He gives you information. He tells you something. But there is more to it than that: he is contending for something. He is taking a position.

To do this, he has to present a reasoned argument. He orders his material, marshals evidence, backs it up with supporting evidence and deductions, and draws conclusions. It is a simple fact that people will listen to someone who tells them what appears to be true, and whose treatment of the subject gets them somewhere. Some modern writers refer to *logos* as 'logical appeal'.

Ethos, pathos, logos—ethical appeal, emotional appeal, logical appeal—all this is very well, but what do these concepts have to do with us, especially in the light of 1 Corinthians 1:17-20 and 2:1-5? These verses read as follows:

> For Christ did not send me to baptize, but to preach the gospel, not with wisdom of words, lest the cross of Christ should be made of no effect. For the message of the cross is foolishness to those who are perishing, but to us who are being saved it is the power of God. For it is written:

'I will destroy the wisdom of the wise,
And bring to nothing the understanding of the prudent.'

Where is the wise? Where is the scribe? Where is the disputer of this age? Has not God made foolish the wisdom of this world?

* * * * *

And I, brethren, when I came to you, did not come with excellence of speech or of wisdom declaring to you the testimony of God. For I determined not to know anything among you except Jesus Christ and him crucified. I was with you in weakness, in fear, and in much trembling. And my speech and my preaching were not with persuasive words of human wisdom, but in demonstration of the Spirit and of power, that your faith should not be in the wisdom of men but in the power of God.'

We will return to these verses shortly but, before we do, I invite you to reflect with me on what Paul says in 1 Thessalonians chapters 1 and 2. In these chapters we see that all three of the characteristics that we are discussing were displayed in Paul's evangelistic and pastoral ministry at Thessalonica.

Paul at Thessalonica

There was *ethos*. Paul and his colleagues were very conscious that their preaching of the gospel would have been hindered if their character had not matched the message they were proclaiming. The credibility of what was said was intimately linked to the integrity of the speakers. 'You know what kind of men we were among you for your sake', Paul writes. 'And you became followers of us and of the Lord' (*1 Thess.* 1:5-6).

Paul is not content to merely talk about this in a general way. He enters into details. 'Our exhortation did not come from deceit or uncleanness, nor was it in guile . . . For neither at any time did we use flattering words, as you know, nor a cloak for covetousness—God is witness . . . You are witnesses, and God also, how devoutly and justly and blamelessly we behaved ourselves among you who believe . . .' (*1 Thess.* 2:,3, 5, 10).

In addition, there was *pathos*. Paul, Silvanus and Timothy felt for the Thessalonians. They begin their letter by wishing them grace and peace (1:1) and by assuring them that they 'give thanks to God always' for every one of them (1:2). They call them 'beloved brethren' (1:4) and show obvious pride in them, because their faith towards God is spoken about everywhere, in such a way that Paul and his band do not need to say anything about them (1:8).

Paul reminds them: 'We were gentle among you, just as a nursing mother cherishes her own children. So, affectionately longing for you, we were well pleased to impart to you not only the gospel of God, but also our own lives, because you had become dear to us' (2:7-8). This *pathos* was one of the factors that God used to open the hearts of the unconverted Thessalonians: 'For this reason we also thank God without ceasing, because when you received the word of God which you heard from us, you welcomed it not as the word of men, but as it is in truth, the word of God, which also effectively works in you who believe' (2:13).

This *pathos* did not desert Paul and his team once they had left Thessalonica. Burning with desire to see their new friends again, they made every effort to return to them as soon as possible (2:17): 'For what is our hope, or joy, or crown of rejoicing? Is it not even you in the presence of our Lord Jesus Christ at his coming? For you are our glory and joy' (2:19-20).

Ethos and *pathos* were accompanied by *logos*. Paul's message had content. He calls that content 'our gospel' (1:5), 'the gospel of God' (2:2), and 'the word of God' (2:13). He sees its content as a sacred deposit with which he and his colleagues have been entrusted by God himself (2:4). Something of its teaching comes across as Paul reminds his readers of the gospel's effect. 'You turned to God from idols', he writes, 'to serve the living and true God, and to wait for his Son from heaven, whom he raised from the dead, even Jesus who delivers us from the wrath to come' (1:9-10).

Ethos, pathos and *logos*—but these three words are not sufficient to fully describe what characterised Paul's ministry at Thessalonica. There was something else—something which is never mentioned by Aristotle or by any other non-Christian writer concerned with the subject of public speaking. It was not an element that we can describe as a mere fourth characteristic. Rather, it was something which both accompanied and permeated the other three and infused them with spiritual power. So what was it?

I shall call it *dunamis*. I have deliberately chosen a Greek word that does not rhyme with the other three, to underline the point that it is not a mere fourth characteristic, but an influence that pervades and saturates the other three. *Dunamis* is the word from which we get our 'dynamite'. It is the wonderful and mighty power by which spiritual work gets done. It is the gentle yet forceful energy of the Holy Spirit.

The conversion of the Thessalonians cannot be explained simply by an appeal to the *ethos, pathos* and *logos* of Paul and his fellow-preachers. Supernatural work must be done by a supernatural power. Such a power affects both preacher and hearer. Paul accounts for what happened at Thessalonica like this:

> Our gospel did not come to you in word only, but also in power (*dunamis*), and in the Holy Spirit, and in much assurance, as you know what kind of men we were among you for your sake. And you became followers of us and of the Lord, having received the word in much affliction, with joy of the Holy Spirit, so that you became examples to all in Macedonia and Achaia who believe.
>
> You turned to God from idols to serve the living and true God, and to wait for his Son from heaven, whom he raised from the dead, even Jesus who delivers us from the wrath to come. . . .
>
> Even after we had suffered before and were spitefully treated at Philippi, as you know, we were bold in our God to speak to you the gospel of God in much conflict . . . When you received the word of God which you heard from us, you welcomed it not as the word of men, but as it is truth, the word of God, which also effectively works in you who believe (1:5-6, 9-10; 2:2, 13).

In Christian history writers have often referred to *dunamis* as 'unction'. E. M. Bounds describes it 'a cordial communication of divine truth' which 'makes God's truth powerful and interesting, draws and attracts, edifies, convicts, saves'. He says that 'this unction vitalizes God's truth, makes it living and life-giving' and 'pervades and convicts the conscience and breaks the heart'. Its effect, he insists, is felt by the preacher as well as the hearer: 'This unction gives to the preacher liberty and enlargement of thought and soul—a freedom, fullness and directness of utterance that can be secured by no other process.'[3]

Other writers have been less specific in trying to define *dunamis*. For example, on 21 June, 1630 at Kirk O'Shotts in Scotland, a large number of people gathered to hear the young preacher John Livingstone. The effect of his sermon was extraordinary and over 500 of them were converted and soon joined gospel-loving churches. Reflecting on this, John Livingstone later wrote:

> There is sometimes somewhat in preaching that cannot be described either to matter or expression, and cannot be described what it is, or from whence it cometh, but with a sweet violence it pierceth into the heart and affections, and comes immediately from the Lord; but if there be any way to obtain such a thing it is by the heavenly disposition of the speaker.[4]

Back to 1 Corinthians

With all this in mind, we are now in a position to return to Paul's statements in 1 Corinthians chapters 1 and 2 and to understand them more fully. The question which is in our mind is quite clear: In what ways, and in what sense, did Paul accept Greek rhetoric; and in what ways, and in what sense, did he reject it entirely?

---

[3] E. M. Bounds, *Power through Prayer* (London, Marshall, Morgan and Scott, undated) pp. 44-48. There are various editions of this work available. All these quotations are from the chapter entitled 'Under the Dew of Heaven'.
[4] Quoted by E. M. Bounds, p. 45.

Ethos was important to him

He valued it, but not because he wished to bolster himself up, to have a reputation, to be admired, or to hear himself praised. These things did not matter to Paul. But integrity mattered a great deal to him and he appealed constantly to his own, as well as to that of his colleagues. This is because integrity is pleasing to God who, after all, is holy. In addition, it saves preachers from hypocrisy, delivers them from being told to practise what they preach, and incarnates (embodies) the life-changing power of the gospel message which the preacher proclaims.

The fact that *ethos* was important to Paul explains his explanations and exhortations elsewhere in the New Testament. For example, it explains why he spends time refuting the possible charge that his failure to come to Rome, as planned, was due to fickleness (*Rom.* 1:13; 15:22). It explains how he can appeal to the Corinthians to learn from his example, and can even go so far as to say to them, 'Imitate me' (*1 Cor.* 9; 4:16; 11:1). It explains why he takes such pains to prove to the same readers that his apostleship is genuine, and does everything possible to convince them of his authority and integrity (see almost all of 2 Corinthians, and especially 6:3-10). It explains why he gives the details about how he received the gospel, and so shows that his message, in contrast to others, is genuine (Galatians).

The value that Paul puts on *ethos* is not seen only in what he says about himself. It propels him to bear witness to the good character of Timothy and Epaphroditus (*Phil.* 2:19-30). It underlies his instructions to Timothy to be as careful about his life as he is to be about the purity of his teaching (*1 Tim.* 4:12-16). It governs his mind as he spells out what qualifications a man must have if he is to serve as an elder or a deacon (*1 Tim.* 3; *Titus* 1:5-9). Paul knew very well that if a man's life is not consistent with his message, there is no place for him in the Christian ministry.

Whether we like it or not, there are such things as 'vibes'. All of us, without exception, arouse feelings in the people with whom we mix. Whether they take us seriously or not is decided by their perception of us. If their emotional response to us convinces them that we do not ring true, they will never listen to us. Of course, people are sinners and they do not always read our 'vibes' accurately. We must be prepared to be misunderstood. But this much is certain: we have no chance of ringing true if we are not true. Our inconsistencies will eventually come to light. The skeletons cannot be kept in the cupboard for ever. Happily, however, in most cases a person with a loving disposition and an impeccable character will eventually be heeded. Who, then, would dare to ignore this question of *ethos*?

Pathos was important to him

It was not the *pathos* of Greek rhetoric that Paul valued. By a variety of tricks that rhetoric set out to manipulate people and to make them compliant. It learned to sway audiences by playing on their emotions. It wept and play-acted, not out of concern for others, but simply for effect. It was self-centred and self-congratulatory.

The existence of counterfeit money only serves to prove the value of genuine currency. Paul's *pathos* was Christlike and sprang out of his feeling for others. Their errors and mistakes plunged him into sorrow and grief. Their spiritual progress filled him with joy. He possessed that deep sincerity which can be sensed and which convinces people that they are listening to an honest man. His whole life and ministry displayed an obvious humanness. In his preaching of the gospel he knew nothing of that 'take it or leave it' attitude which characterises heartless hirelings.

How important such a *pathos* was to him can be seen in any number of New Testament passages. Have you ever thought about the greetings which open his letters, or the benedictions which bring them to a close? His loving heart overflows with his 'Grace to you and peace from God our Father and the Lord Jesus Christ' (*Rom.* 1:7). He cannot end his letters without a 'Now the God of peace be with you all' (*Rom.* 15:33) or something similar, and his written prayer that Christ's grace should be with his readers is his personal signature tune (*Rom.* 16:20, 24; *2 Thess.* 3:16-18).

To Paul, all his converted readers are his 'brethren' who, to him, are 'beloved'. To those whom he has never met, or has been separated from, he writes, 'I long to see you . . . that I may be encouraged together with you' (*Rom.* 1:11-12). Although he longs to be in the immediate presence of Christ, he is confident of remaining on earth as a means of continuing blessing to the Philippians, because 'to remain in the flesh is more needful for you' (*Phil.* 1:24). He is a man with a big heart, and he gives that heart to whomever he meets. This is why people wept openly when they had to say goodbye to him (*Acts* 20:36-38; *2 Tim.* 1:4). His deep affection bound them to him. Who, then, would ever consider ignoring this question of *pathos*?

Logos was important to him

The *logos* that Paul valued was not the one that was so idolised by the Greek rhetoricians. They saw public speaking as a way of commanding admiration. In their circles a speaker would be congratulated for his skill in choosing certain words, his choice of arguments suitable to the occasion and the hearers, his ability to marshal his arguments to the greatest effect, as well as his intonation, pronunciation, modulation, and everything else that makes the voice attractive.

The *logos* that Paul treasured was that which makes the only saving gospel clear to people. It tells them what they are to believe concerning God and what duty he requires of them. In this *logos* nothing is hidden, obscure or ambiguous. It gives reasons and it answers objections. It points unbelievers to salvation by faith in Christ alone, and leads the Lord's people into the paths of holiness and comfort.

It is this *logos* that underlies the logical development and argument of Paul's Epistles to the Romans and Galatians, the sustained and thorough answering of questions in 1 Corinthians, and the time spent in 2 Corinthians and Colossians in defending vulnerable believers from error. In Ephesians it sets to instruct readers in their privileges, while in 1 Thessalonians it is concerned with comforting them. Everything that Paul speaks or writes has content. There is nothing superficial about it. It is faithful to God and useful to others. Seeing that such a *logos* exists, who is the preacher who would not want to know more about it?

Dunamis was important to him

The concept of *dunamis* was unknown in Greek rhetoric. The ancient orators thought that if you did not manage to convince your hearers, it was because you had not fully mastered the art of persuasion. They had no notion of sin as taught in the Word of God, and therefore no understanding of spiritual death and of the need of a spiritual resurrection. They knew nothing of the new birth. Regeneration was not a subject that they ever considered.

The importance of *dunamis* to Paul is not only seen in the passages in 1 Corinthians and 1 Thessalonians which we have already quoted, but is evident both explicitly and implicitly throughout his writings. It is in his mind all the time. This is why he repeatedly refers to the fact that he prays for those who are reading his letters. He also reveals the content of those prayers—basically he is constantly asking that God himself will do something in the hearts and lives of his readers. His ministry is governed by the conviction that men can both sow and water the seed of the Word, but that only God can give life to that seed (*1 Cor.* 3:6). In Paul, just as in the case of the earlier apostles, we see that his practice is that of Acts 6:4: 'We will give ourselves continually to prayer and to the ministry of the Word'—in that order!

Those early apostles understood that it is better to default on every other responsibility than it is to neglect prayer. Communion with God even takes precedence over the ministry of the Word. Compared with prayer, preaching is only an *'and'*. It must never take first place. Prayer recognises God as God, and depends on him to do what he would not without prayer. Prayer, and prayer alone, is the way by which the Lord's armies call him onto the field.

Martyn Lloyd-Jones, too, lived by this principle. He was primarily a man of prayer, and only then a preacher, as are all (without exception) who value *dunamis*. How else could *dunamis* be obtained? Thank God for his promises in this regard:

> And all things, whatever you ask in prayer, believing, you will receive (*Matt.* 21:22).

> If you then, being evil, know how to give good gifts to your children, how much more will your heavenly Father give the Holy Spirit to those who ask him! (*Luke* 11:13).

> And whatever you ask in my name, that will I do, that the Father may be glorified in the Son. If you ask anything in my name, I will do it (*John* 14:13-14).

We must have the Holy Spirit! There was no preaching, in the full New Testament sense, until he descended at Pentecost. The disciples spent more than three years with the Lord Jesus Christ, but this did not make preachers out of them. They heard his teaching and observed his miracles. Three of them witnessed both his transfiguration and his bloodied agony in the Garden of Gethsemane. They saw the cross, the blood, the resurrection appearances and the ascension but, to become preachers, they had to wait until they were 'endued with power from on high' (*Luke* 24:49). This does not mean that they afterwards prayed for a new Pentecost every time that they preached, but they knew that without the immediate and direct blessing of God they would remain powerless, and that nothing of spiritual value would ever get done. It is not a surprise to us, therefore, to read later on:

> And when they had prayed, the place where they were assembled together was shaken; and they were all filled with the Holy Spirit, and they spoke the word of God with boldness (*Acts* 4:31).

Dunamis permeates *ethos, pathos* and *logos*. This is confirmed, for example, by a brief look at the ministry of Stephen. *Ethos:* Stephen was a Spirit-filled man who was known for his good reputation and wisdom. His opponents were not able to withstand the wisdom and the Spirit by which he spoke (*Acts* 6:3, 10). *Pathos:* he was a man who loved his hearers, as is proved by his moving prayer for them while they stoned him to death (*Acts* 7:60). *Logos:* as he preached, his explanation of the Scriptures revealed that he had unusual spiritual insight. Even today his magnificent sermon in Acts chapter 7 takes our breath away. It was this sermon, it seems, which was the foundation for the whole of Paul's future understanding and spiritual development.

We must have *dunamis!* If we do not, our *ethos, pathos* and *logos* will be nothing, as far as real spiritual work is concerned. It is perfectly all right for us to stress these three elements, but it is essential that we also stress that they cannot bear spiritual fruit unless they are permeated with the sanctifying power of the Holy Spirit.

Who, who, will give himself to prayer, that their preaching (or the preaching of the man that they pray for) may be 'in demonstration of the Spirit and of power'? (*1 Cor.* 2:4). Who will wrestle with God, saying to him, 'I will not let you go unless you bless me'? (*Gen.* 32:26). Who for spiritual results will decide to rely on God alone, and to rely on him completely? Who will remain unsatisfied, until it is said of their ministry what was said of Jacob: 'And [the Lord] blessed him there'? (*Gen.* 32:29).

3. UPSIDE-DOWN THINKING

At this point I want to introduce you to what we call 'Upside-Down Thinking'. It is a way of helping people to think more clearly about something that they are working through in their minds.

To do this, let me introduce you to the Poppitti family, whose members run a restaurant. The restaurant is doing badly and all the family members get together to see what can be done about it. To help them do this, Papa Poppitti decides not to ask them what they can do to make their restaurant a success. The question he puts to them is: 'What can we do to make our restaurant a failure?'

In a similar situation, what answer would you give to that question? You might come up with suggestions such as these:

• Make the restaurant look as run-down as possible, so that everyone will think that it is closed.

• Only open at times when people do not want to eat.

• Make it almost impossible for customers to work out how to get their cars into the car park and, if they succeed, make it equally difficult for them to find the restaurant entrance.

• Ignore everyone who comes in.

• Have tatty menus, dirty table-cloths and stained cutlery.

• Ensure that nobody pays any attention to customers who sit at table.

• Serve awful food.

• Charge exorbitant prices . . .

Once the Poppitti family members had given their answers, they quickly understood how to improve their restaurant. They simply had to do the opposite of what they had suggested! For some reason or other (it is probably to do with the Fall) most people find it easier to think in the negative. Upside-Down Thinking helps us to clear our minds and to see the issues more clearly. This being so, let us apply it to the whole question of preaching.

What can a preacher do to make sure that he does not get through?

[1] *Ethos (Ethical appeal)*

Here the golden rule is: *Keep your distance from people!*

Do not give your hearers any real opportunity of getting to know you, and be especially careful not to mix with people whom they may know, in case they get information about you that way.

Do not visit your hearers in their homes, and certainly never have them into your own home. Keep away from their places of work. Do not mingle with them either before or after services—the way to do this is to arrive as late as possible at church, and to leave as soon as you can afterwards.

Do not make any references to yourself in your sermons—ever! In short, make sure that those who hear you know as little as possible about you. Build up no empathy with them and no ties of affection. Just stand up at the front and give people messages!

In this way no one will ever have any clue as to whether your life matches your teaching or not. They will simply not know whether you practise what you preach, and so you will be spared the embarrassment of people appealing to your personal example. Nor will they have any idea as to whether you really know what you are talking about, because they will know nothing of your life, your studies, your reading, your experience or your expertise.

In addition, you will be spared the effort of living a life of integrity, honesty, purity and discretion, because no one will be in a position to catch you out. Nor will you have to engage in the iron self-discipline that is necessary for a growing devotional life, with its cultivation of goodness, knowledge, courage, zeal, sincerity, passion, faith, prayer and consistent personal holiness.

The result will be that you will fail to incarnate (embody) the life-changing power of the message that you preach. You will have no moral authority. You will send out no helpful 'vibes'. Nor will you have any experience of *dunamis*. Your hypocrisy will eventually be discovered, and you will never get through to anyone again.

[2] *Pathos (Emotional appeal)*

Here the golden rule is: *Show no feeling!*

There are two sorts of feeling—feeling about what you are preaching, and feeling for the people you are speaking to. Make sure that you do not display either one or the other!

It is said that C. H. Spurgeon's success was largely due to the fact that he was 'absorbed with his audience'. At all costs, avoid his example. Just get through your material and then hurry home. Do not leave people with the slightest impression that you want to do them good and that you care about them. Be particularly careful not to use any kind or affectionate words in both public preaching and personal conversation.

Make no attempt to put yourself in your hearers' shoes. Do nothing to arouse them. Do not make it easy for them to listen to you. Choose words and concepts that ordinary people will find difficult to grasp. Steer clear of all illustrations that might help them, especially stories. Forget that people have imaginations and never appeal to this faculty. Be careful also about applications, in case they pick up the idea that what you are saying is relevant to their daily lives, and is something to be lived out.

Never get worked up or moved by anything that you say, unless it is clearly to your advantage—in which case you should sway their emotions without mercy and manipulate them in every way you can. Show no grief for your hearers' mistakes and no joy over their spiritual progress. Display no humanness, in case you put yourself in a position where you are in some way vulnerable. And certainly never give them the idea that there is anything that they can do which would encourage you!

Finally, in this section, if they do not like or understand what you are saying, tell them to 'like it or lump it'.

[3] Logos (Logical appeal)

Here the golden rule is: *Do not work too hard!*

Why should you? Is it not your ambition that they should learn as little as possible? And why should you bother to get your exegesis exactly right, to order your thoughts, to reason through an argument, to back up anything you say, and to come to a conclusion? Come on now, get a life! Forget all that hard work.

Tell your hearers the truth, yes; but never in a way that stimulates any thought. Treat every truth alike. Never give them the impression that some truths are more important than others; in other words, never focus on those fundamental truths that some people call 'the gospel'.

Give no reasons. Answer no questions. Do not call people to any duties. Never draw out for them any comfort. Do not point them to any blessings. Just leave all that you say in the abstract, unrelated to anyone's lives or feelings.

If everything you say remains obscure and unclear—one indigestible lump of propositions with nothing attractive or appealing about it, delivered without gesture or animation, with a voice that is as monotonous as the background drone of a bagpipe—you will have done well. You will get through to nobody!

To make entirely sure of this, cast entirely out of your mind the uncomfortable truth that you will one day personally answer to God for every word that you have spoken, and that, as a teacher of his church, you will 'receive a stricter judgment' (*James* 3:1). Do not think about it! Rather, think like this: As long as there are people in the congregation, what else could possibly matter?

[4] *Dunamis (Supernatural accompaniment)*

Here the golden rule is: *Ignore this dimension altogether!*

Countless preachers show no interest in the subject, so why should you? After all, there has been a lot of debate about the exact meaning of the passages in 1 Thessalonians 1:5 and 1 Corinthians 2:4, so why get involved?

Besides, if it is true that only God can give life to the seed, he is going to do that whether you or anybody else thinks about *dunamis* or not. Do you really want to be accused of being a mystic?

And as for all that praying, just remember that we live in the twenty-first century. There are just not enough hours in a day to even consider such an expenditure of time and energy. What about all your other responsibilities?

Forget the concept of being 'endued with power from on high' (*Luke* 24:49). Do not give yourself a bad conscience because of your lack of prayer in this area. The concept is simply not definite enough to get worked up about; the work of God has gone ahead throughout the world without most preachers ever giving attention to the question of unction. The safest course of action for you, and the simplest, is in the golden rule above: *Ignore this dimension altogether!*

* * * * *

What can a preacher do to make sure that he does not get through? We have considered four areas and have come up with four golden rules:

1. *Ethos* [Ethical appeal]: Keep your distance from people!
2. *Pathos* [Emotional appeal]: Show no feeling!
3. *Logos* [Logical appeal]: Do not work too hard!
4. *Dunamis* [Supernatural accompaniment]: Ignore this dimension altogether!

As we went through these four points, were you able to think upside-down? If so, you will know what all of us preachers have to do. If you are not a preacher, you will now have a good idea of what you have to do to help us.

We have caught sight of the ocean, even if we have not explored it. Hopefully then, as we come to the end of this booklet, all of us can understand a little more of what has to be considered in any reflection on *Preaching that Gets Through—God's Word and our words*. Thank you for reading this modest contribution to the subject, and please get in touch with me via the publisher if you would like to pursue the matter further.

Other booklets in this series from
The Banner of Truth Trust:

Abortion: Open Your Mouth for the Dumb *Peter Barnes*
The Authentic Gospel *Jeffrey Wilson*
Behind a Frowning Providence *John J. Murray*
The Bleeding of the Evangelical Church *David Wells*
Burial or Cremation? Does It Matter? *Donald Howard*
A Call to Prayer *J. C. Ryle*
Can We Know God? *Maurice Roberts*
The Carnal Christian *Ernest Reisinger*
Christians Grieve Too *Donald Howard*
Coming to Faith in Christ *John Benton*
The Cross: the Pulpit of God's Love *Iain H. Murray*
The Cross: the Vindication of God *D. M. Lloyd-Jones*
A Defence of Calvinism *C. H. Spurgeon*
Evangelistic Calvinism *John Benton*
The Five Points of Calvinism *W. J. Seaton*
The Free Offer of the Gospel *John Murray*
Healthy Christian Growth *Sinclair B. Ferguson*
Her Husband's Crown *Sara Leone*
Holiness *Joel R. Beeke*
The Incomparable Book *W. J. McDowell*
The Invitation System *Iain H. Murray*
Jesus Christ and Him Crucified *D. M. Lloyd-Jones*
The Kingdom of God *W. Tullian Tchividjian*

A Life of Principled Obedience *A. N. Martin*
Living the Christian Life *A. N. Martin*
The Practical Implications of Calvinism *A. N. Martin*
Preaching: The Centrality of Scripture *R. Albert Mohler*
The Priority of Preaching *John Cheeseman*
The Psalter – the Only Hymnal? *Iain H. Murray*
Read Any Good Books? *Sinclair B. Ferguson*
Reading the Bible *Geoffrey Thomas*
Reading the Bible and Praying in Public *Stuart Olyott*
Rest in God *Iain H. Murray*
Simplicity in Preaching *J. C. Ryle*
Study Guide for 'The Mortification of Sin' *Rob Edwards*
Study Guide for 'The Promise of the Future' *Cornelis P. Venema*
The Unresolved Controversy *Iain H. Murray*
Victory: The Work of the Spirit *Pieter Potgieter*
What Is the Reformed Faith? *J. R. de Witt*
What's Wrong with Preaching Today? *A. N. Martin*
Whom Shall I Marry? *Andrew Swanson*
Worship *J. C. Ryle*

For details of other helpful publications
please visit our website.

THE BANNER OF TRUTH TRUST

3 Murrayfield Road,
Edinburgh EH12 6EL
UK

P O Box 621, Carlisle,
Pennsylvania 17013,
USA

www.banneroftruth.co.uk